In Search of the Great Dead

CRAB ORCHARD AWARD SERIES IN POETRY

Crab Orchard Review **&** Southern Illinois University Press

In Search of the Great Dead

RICHARD CECIL

CARBONDALE AND EDWARDSVILLE

Printed in the United States of America

02   01   00   99   4   3   2   1

Library of Congress Cataloging-in-Publication Data

Cecil, Richard, 1944–
In search of the great dead / Richard Cecil.
p.   cm.   —   (Crab Orchard award series in poetry)
I. Title.   II. Series.
PS3553.E3215 1999
811'.54—dc21   98-40993
ISBN 0-8093-2260-9 (alk. paper)   CIP

The paper used in this publication meets the minimum requirements
of American National Standard for Information Sciences—
Permanence of Paper for Printed Library Materials, ANSI Z39.48-
1984. ⊗

The Crab Orchard Award Series in Poetry is a joint publishing venture
of Southern Illinois University Press and *Crab Orchard Review*. This
series has been made possible by the generous support of the Office of
the President of Southern Illinois University and the Office of the Vice
Chancellor for Academic Affairs and Provost at Southern Illinois
University at Carbondale.

Crab Orchard Award Series in Poetry Editor: Jon Tribble
Judge for 1998: Rodney Jones

For Maura, Olive, and Oleander

Contents

Acknowledgments

Poems in this collection have appeared in the following magazines:

American Poetry Review—"Caliban and Ariel," "*La Notte*"

American Scholar—"Incident at Third and Woodlawn"

Arts Indiana—"Do It Yourself," "Dressing for Work," "Life at the Top"

Crab Orchard Review—"Picnic in the Basement"

Crazyhorse—"Adult Education," "The Education of a Professor," "How Fiction Ruined My Life," "Front Porch Visiting," "In Memoriam," "Life Is like a Mountain Railway," "A Portrait of the Artist's Bedroom," "Room with View/Radio," "Slow Poison," "Thanatopsis," "The Wedding of M & R," "This Train Isn't Bound for Glory"

Dominion Review—"Narcissus Experiences Technical Difficulties"

Georgia Review—"Authors in Hell"

Hopewell Review—"Charlie Chan Solves Another Murder," "Living in Obscurity"

Illinois Review—"My Muse"

Nebraska Review—"Arrivals"

New England Review—"The Thinkers"

North Dakota Quarterly—"Angel Sighted from Airliner!"

Ploughshares—"In Search of the Great Dead," "Why I Have No Children"

Poetry—"A Saint's Life"

Widener Review—"The Little Prince"

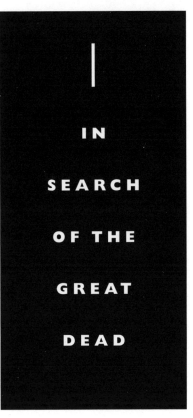

I

IN

SEARCH

OF THE

GREAT

DEAD

In Search of the Great Dead

In Paris, Vallejo's hotel
near the Bibliothèque Nationale
charges a hundred a night,
and Ginsberg's seedy room
on the rue Git-le-coeur
sports flowered wallpaper now,
and a couple of Michelin stars.
Cabourg's Grand Hotel
on the chilly Normandy coast,
nearly driven from business
by the sunny "costas" of Spain,
rents "Chambre Marcel Proust"
for twice the price of a suite—
a week's pay for the profs
who book it, months in advance,
to lie in Proust's bed one night
fighting sleep as they read
his description of insomnia
in his snail-paced masterpiece.
And, speaking of Spain, in Ronda
Rilke slept for a month
in room 208
of the Reina Victoria Hotel,
which exhibits souvenirs—
some scribbles, a cancelled bill—
that cold man left behind
when he resumed his search
for gorgeous emptiness
hollow as his hollow heart.
But if their names have jacked
ridiculously the rent
of the tiny, outmoded rooms
they slept in for pocket change,
like the "Taube" in Hemingway's Shruns,
now a first class Austrian Inn
with a three-color brochure

where, for $2.50 a night,
he polished *The Sun Also Rises,*
abandoned his wife for his mistress,
and blamed it all on Dos Passos—
consider visiting their tombs.

In Cimetière Père-Lachaise
in Paris you can stand
for nothing by Alice B. Toklas's
and Gertrude Stein's remains
and stare at their blank stone—
not a single word but their names
after thousands of pages of chatter!
From their excellent address
in the capital city of death,
avenues of genius
fan in all directions.
But if you prefer the lonely
and isolated dead,
Chateaubriand in St-Malo
on an island linked to the mainland
for an hour at ebb tide
rests within the sound
of the wind and the sea—and the tourists
who photograph his inscription
quick! before the causeway floods.
Then they board the ferry
to the sullen Irish coast
to add William Butler Yeats
to their album of poet's tombs.
Graves's grave's in Majorca
near the Chopin/Sand Condominiums;
Dante's is in Ravenna,
Keats's and Shelley's in Rome,
where poets and Caesars lie
whose marble cenotaphs
barbarians burned for lime.
Augustus paid Virgil and Horace
to praise his empire and Virtue,

then Nero slaughtered Lucan
for winning a poetry contest,
and Seneca for hating vice,
but all of their tombs are lost.
There is no place to stand
feeling your heart expand
at the greatness of the waste
that lies between you and them;
at the brilliance of their lines
through centuries of gloom
overshadowing patronage
and hostility alike.
First the houses they lived in,
then their houses of death
disappeared, and all that's left
are their works—some of their works—
some fragment of their works.
Half of Livy's *History,*
the juiciest parts of Tacitus
were ripped out, charred, scraped off
to make paper for another bible
or wipe the ass of a monk.
All that's left of Sappho
is several hundred words
caught drifting on the wind
from the fire at Alexandria,
and *Gilgamesh,* written on stone,
is written on pebbles now—
pebbles displayed like diamonds
for crowds at the British Museum.

When the pebbles become grains of sand
and blow away in the wind
of a nuclear strike on London
or the gentler breeze of erosion
after the city's abandoned,
that epic's only remnant
will be Hatred of Death,
which is the theme of *Gilgamesh*

and also the impulse that drove
its author to hack it in granite.
"Now I'll never die,"
he said to himself as he wiped
his bleeding hands on his shirt.
And he hasn't, quite, yet,
though bombs from the War for Oil
rocked his ancient, anonymous bones
recently and will again.
The little wars and the Big One
the lovers of death are planning
will leave no monuments
but rubble and rows and columns
of identical soldiers' tombs
next to the fields and trees
or featureless, shifting dunes
that thousands of *x*s and *y*s
died for, not guessing why,
and the unmarked humps of mass graves
of civilians who got in the way.
These, too, attract their visitors,
veterans and survivors
who've vowed never to forget,
and, later, politicians
for a century or two, but at last
only the haters of death
walk these bone yard acres
shaking their heads and digging
their nails into their palms,
driving needles of pain
up their arms into their brains
to shake the drowsy numbness
of so much nameless slaughter,
exactly like the numbness
that comes, reading Livy's *History*
in bed, late at night.
10,000 Carthaginians
slaughtered 10,000 Romans
in 300 B.C. or vice versa—

annihilating armies
annihilated in turn
until the Empire, secured,
turned upon itself
and Romans murdered Romans—
fathers, sons, brothers—
for four more hundred years.
Their civil war graveyards,
long buried by barbarians,
must once have looked like ours
at Fredericksburg and Shiloh,
where every numbered marker
listing Company and Regiment
whispers, like Emily Dickinson,
"I'm Nobody—are you
Nobody, too?"

        Oh, yes,
I'm Nobody, too. My plot,
reserved for a small down payment
at Valhalla Memory Gardens,
isn't a pilgrimage site;
it's not on the tour bus route,
not topped with a simple stone
carved with memorable words,
waiting, impatient, for me
to die to make them immortal.
My house, 912 East First,
lacks a bronze inscription
screwed into its plastic siding
and will certainly be converted
to a rental, not a museum
when I leave it dead or, alive,
determined to die in Florida
or Southern France, like Yeats,
desiring a year in the sun
after a lifetime of gloom
and greenness and peasant neighbors.
That year's when I plan to write

my deathless epitaph
and enter it in the contest
glutted with Baby Boom poets
dying at the rate they were born.
But first, I'll waste my life,
like now, writing against
the grain of drowsiness—
I rose at 4 A.M.—
with Olive, my black and white cat,
kneading my arm with her claws—
a pleasure so much like pain,
a pain so much like pleasure,
like dying after a long illness,
then haunting the house you lived in,
brushing the fabrics you touched,
shoving ghostly feet into shoes,
marveling at their size and weight,
in which you once walked like a giant.
For even the greatest dead,
if death isn't just dirt in the mouth,
must moan with their reedy voices
for the life they lost to be famous.

La Notte

I barged into a crowded room
angrily searching for a phone
to place a call to an old friend
who'd passed me on the grounds outside,
shrugging and turning away when I waved.
But when I lifted the receiver
a stranger in an evening gown
shook her head and tapped the ear piece
with her long black fingernails.
Someone was chatting on the line
in what sounded like Italian.
I hung up and stepped outside
through glass French doors into the garden
where couples strolled on lighted paths
or sipped champagne in semi-darkness
by the fountain whose loud plashing
made it hard to overhear them.
Below the tinkle of false laughter
I heard the low hum of real grief
as one couple talked in whispers
while she shredded wadded kleenex
and her partner rattled change
deep in his tuxedo pocket.
Death or divorce must be their subject,
I guessed as I edged closer to them,
but when I got in hearing range,
the man receded in the shadows,
looking for his wife or mistress,
leaving the woman alone and weeping.
Shaken by her sobs, a strap
from her black silk cocktail dress
slipped from her shoulder. *Scusa signora*
I ached to say as I reached to fix it,
but paralysis gripped my arm and throat.
She plucked it nervously back in place
on the softest marbly white skin on earth,

then walked through me, into the night.
I saw, then, that I had no substance
as well as no voice—I was a ghost
among rich, beautiful, black and white ghosts
whose sadness moved me more than my sadness
at being ignored by my once loved friend.
What was she doing in my dream,
I wondered as I fought to stay under
the surface of my unconsciousness.
I knew that waking, I'd remember the movie
by Antonioni or Fellini
I saw with my friend when we were young
and trembled with passion, like the starlet,
not suspecting that it was false,
while the shallow, bored sophistication
of the minor roles would fall to us
starring in the films of our separate lives.

In Memoriam

for Lynda Hull

Wires bowed with snow sway from the power pole.
Somewhere down the street, a fuse explodes.
Lights flicker and go out, then on again,
then out for good, and lines I just keyed in

have disappeared off of my laptop's screen
and sunk, unsaved, to the Limbo of electrons
which, half a second ago, bunched into letters,
but scatter, now, like ions through a cloud chamber.

To find them and reform them into words
I'll have to tunnel back to where they paused
an instant in my brain's network of nerves
and read ghost images they faintly etched

into the walls of my short-term memory
before they streaked off toward oblivion
at the universe's edge at the speed of light.
To concentrate on searching for their tracks,

I plug my ears against the moaning wind
after I switch off my useless laptop
and replace it with a pen and pad of paper
propped on my knees, ready to take down

whatever I haul up from my descent.
New thoughts brush by me, but I shrink from them;
I mean to think of just the lines snatched from me
and dragged below right after they were born.

I feel my way into my memory,
whose walls are crudely crayoned with graffiti.
I must be in the long-term antechamber,
where the broken furniture of childhood's piled.

I scramble through the jumble of stuffed toys
which, if I pause, will swamp me with nostalgia.
There's Teddy leaking stuffing! There's Rudolf, de-nosed,
his antlers drooping from frayed threads and . . . No!

Beyond the anteroom, the cave expands.
Its ceiling glows with blue fluorescent light
which illuminates high rows of file cabinets
crammed with labeled folders full of facts,

such as what temperature turns rain to sleet
and causes cars to spin out, as mine did
twenty years ago, which nearly killed me,
and which killed Lynda two years ago exactly.

Today's the anniversary of her death
in late March, when rain froze, just like today,
except today it freezes miles above
the wires and branches that it's tearing down

and piles so high that it imprisons cars
in driveways, and their owners, trapped inside
their cold, dark houses, curse their immobility.
Two years ago, they could have sped, like her,

at eighty miles per hour into a tree,
and have their ashes scattered three days later,
and even the day they died be half forgotten
after a couple of spins of the Season's wheel.

Be patient. Lineman have been climbing poles
and city road crews plowing drifts all night,
and though they fail to keep up with the storm,
April's coming to sweep it up for them.

Whan that April with his showres soote
melts icicles dangling from our roofs,

and lights and furnaces click on again,
I'll forget my friend died in cold rain

March 29, 1994
unless I write it down with pen and paper
in lines shaped by the ghost of rhyme and meter—
not the lost lines I descended for,

which glowed an instant longer than my thought,
and then flamed out in my mind's cave, extinguished
by ice's touch, just like my young friend Lynda,
whose brilliant lines burn on and on without her.

On the Observation Platform

The plane I'm watching for is late.
Each time the P.A. speakers crackle,
I brace to hear a grim announcement:
"Will those awaiting Flight Thirteen
please come to the Departure Lounge?"
Though flying's safe and driving's not,

I do not grip my window sill
and watch, white knuckled, when my wife
shifts into Drive and enters traffic;
and when I cinch my car's seat belt,
my life's mistakes and old regrets
do not parade past my mind's eye.

I fell asleep on the Channel ferry
that once drowned hundreds in the harbor,
and I've napped on high speed trains
whose engineers drink wine with lunch,
and yawned, bored, on mountain buses
turning blind through horseshoe bends.

How come I don't trust U.S. Air
the way I trusted Paraguayan
boatmen on the Paraná River,
who rowed me to the brink of falls
at Iguassú, that dwarf Niagara?
Speaking of Niagara Falls,

why did I thrill with joy, not terror,
when soused with spray from the Bridal Veil
while leaning from *Maid of the Mist*'s railing?
I don't think instinct is the answer,
since instinct tells me water drowns
and that cars cross land much too fast.

Instinct ordered me to freeze
last August when I laughed and mounted
The World's Fastest Roller Coaster.
I couldn't plead necessity
to get somewhere when I locked the bar
across my lap and thrilled with fear—

a silver shiver in my veins
like the first sip of a martini
as my car ratcheted uphill.
But when a jet begins to taxi
with me strapped in, lead clogs my blood
no matter where or why I'm flying,

and when someone I can't bear losing's
late returning from the clouds
she winged into for money, fame,
or to visit distant parents,
every reason's frivolous
for leaving me alone on earth

until I think I see—I do!
the plane that I've been watching for,
and press my face hard to the glass
to beam the pilot in to touchdown—
a spectacularly routine landing
I'm silently but wildly cheering.

The Autobiography of My House

"There goes the neighborhood,"
the watchers at their windows
groaned when Allied Movers
rolled the cat-clawed couch
down the loading ramp.
Next door, the widow sighed
stroking Figaro,
her silver Persian cat,
while on the other side,
frowning Mrs. Smith
scanned the dusty lamps
and dented appliances
scattered around the sidewalk
looking for amplifiers
and oversized stereo speakers.
Out back, a very old lady
stared at the dinette's
ripped blue vinyl chairs
and decided to reconsider
her pushy grandson's advice
to move to Meadowood,
"a minimum care facility."
Out front, on the boulevard,
up in the maple branches
brushed by the top of the van,
robins and chickadees
click-clicked in dismay.
They guessed this seedy stuff
belonged to the kind of people
who wouldn't re-hang the feeder
un-hung by the people who left.
Their bread crumbs flung on the snow,
their suet hung from the eaves
were things of the past.
Even the grass complained
(although the weeds rejoiced)

when the rusty, hand-pushed mower
wheeled into the garage.
No more Weed & Feed
applications in the spring,
no insecticidal baths
once a month in summer.
The oak planks trembled
when movers mounted the stairs
with battered wardrobe boxes
and a heavy metal desk.
The polished hardwood floor
of the living room reflected
a plastic coffee table
for the first time in its life,
and the kitchen's microwave shelf
gaped, vacant as a gum
after it loses a tooth.
"We're coming down in life,"
whined fleas caught napping in the rug
when their host pets moved out,
as Allied's men set down
the stainless steel pedestal
of the maple table
on patches of carpet worn napless
by solid mahogany feet.

But the study's built-in shelves,
bowed by legal textbooks,
felt relief at the lightness
of skinny paperbacks,
and the somber, dark green bedroom
cheered up when painted white.
In a week the nervous birds
grew used to the indoor cats
who watched them from front windows
when they pecked at the dogwood's berries
and dug grubs out of gutters.
After a month of silence—
no parties no laughter no music—

the neighbors began to relax.
In a year, a near-tornado
blew away the maple,
replaced by a Bradford Pear,
which flourished like the weeds
in the poorly tended yard.
It blossomed white each Easter,
and its dark green leaves turned red
as ornaments in late November
and hung on branches till Christmas
when they fell in glittering heaps.
The old lady died;
the Smiths' house doubled in size;
the widow grew older and sadder;
and everybody forgot
the people who moved away
long ago to a better house
and their children—by now, adults.
But those children dream, sometimes,
they're sleeping in the west bedroom
with the yellow animal wallpaper
the new people didn't paint white
when they painted everything else.
Lions, giraffes, mice,
kangaroos and elephants
still dance around the walls
of this room where cats now sleep,
dreaming their paw-twitching dreams
of opening their Christmas presents
heavily spiced with catnip
wrapped under the tree downstairs.
But the grown up dreaming children
wake to indifferent ceilings
and strangers sleeping beside them,
and remember all they've lost.
For them each waking's a move
to a dingier neighborhood.
And what are the "new" owners dreaming?
Of houses they could afford

now that they've paid the mortgage?
That would explain the moaning
coming from the husband's lips
as Allied's van pulls up
painted, not orange, but black,
and the movers in black suits
lift him by his head and feet
and trundle him up the ramp
with all of his shabby stuff
for a ride down the one-way street.
Once more, the rooms rest vacant,
unburdened of furniture,
waiting for the new tenants
to drag the neighborhood down
while the watchers at the windows
twitch their arthritic fingers
to close their curtains of gauze.

This Train Isn't Bound for Glory

Can't sleep. The neighbors have grown too quiet.
Old dogs don't bark at the moon anymore,
and teens who left in noisy jalopies
return at Christmas in family cars
with "Baby on Board" tags stuck to windows
obstructed with blankets and Teddy Bears,

just as they did in the neighborhood
where I grew up and longed to escape.
But Ann and Rick in the corner house
got out before me—though I didn't envy
Ann when she entered a nunnery,
or Rick when he married and joined the Army.

Lounging, Sundays, on my childhood porch,
I'd duck behind the funny papers
so as not to have to say "Hi!" to Rick
when he pulled up in his Chevy wagon
with his tiny wife and little brood,
in his Second Lieutenant's uniform,

and I shuddered when I thought of Sister Ann.
By now she must be a Mother Superior,
like Rosalind Russell in *The Trouble with Angels*,
converting feisty convent school girls
like Haley Mills into Servants of God.
That movie's been playing in my head all night.

Why didn't I switch it off while Haley
and her friend smoked stogies in the boiler room?
That's when I glimpsed their future approaching
like a locomotive, coming to crush them—
to mangle Haley into a nun
and her dumb friend into a mother.

"Watch out!" I groaned at my flickering screen.
But even if I could have saved them
for the Big Party that had just begun—
sex without babies, nuns chucking their veils—
I couldn't have slowed that unstoppable train
that rolled over Rosalind decades ago;

that's hauling Haley, her friend, and me
now through the valley of middle age.
Watching the dead level winter landscape
through smudgy panes puts some to sleep,
like uncurious cats curled in the windows
of the large, dull middle class houses we pass,

but not me. My face is pressed to the glass
between me and that darkening scene.
I've added no children to the playgrounds
we rumble by, picking up steam.
Their puppies, unbought, haven't barked all night
for a dozen years, then suddenly stopped

leaving behind a vacuum of silence
the bitter wind whistling past fills in.
At 25,000 miles per hour,
our boxcar houses are dragged through the dark—
are you with us, Mother Ann? and Colonel Rick?—
towards Nowhere by No One, our Engineer.

Charlie Chan Solves Another Murder

In suits, fedoras, identical mustaches,
in feathered hats, white gloves, and tailored dresses,
his suspects mill beneath the chandelier
exchanging furtive glances. They grin or sneer
when he addresses them in Pidgin English
larded with quotations from Confucius,
who says, "grammar like electric eel—
respect greatly, but can not grasp." He'll
twirl his bowler in his meaty hands
as if confused, but don't be fooled—Chan's
already pierced the mystery. He knows who
killed the corpse and how. "Was it you, or you?"
the camera asks each bland, young face it pans—
grade B actors and actresses whose plans
to break into Features and out of Detective Series
are barely concealed as they blurt their theories
concerning the crime: "He knew the gun was loaded,"
says the woman in black. "I didn't, but his widow did,"
replies the shady lawyer. One by one,
they finger each other, while Chan's number 2 son,
a dunce whose UCLA accent proves
that college is a waste of Pop's money, moves
from accused to accused brandishing keyless handcuffs
he's fated to snare himself with, like Oedipus.
Frowning, Charlie thinks, *offspring of genius*
seldom genius. But he mustn't say this,
for his role's to play modest while his son plays witless,
and each suspect acts innocent in a guilty way,
so that, when Chan points out the woman in gray,
whose nervous smile turns instantly into a snarl,
I'm not surprised, although I thought it was Karl,
the Nazi chauffeur who looks a little like Gable.
The men all do. And the women all look like Grable.
Or did when this was filmed a half-century ago.
And do still now, I'm afraid, encoffined below
the raped and butchered landscape of L.A.

Stalked for decades, they were caught alone one day
and rubbed out. Bad actors. Failed artists. Done
in by the serial killer, Oblivion.
Oh god, I hear his footsteps on my stair!
He's here beside me, leaning on my bedroom chair,
smiling inscrutably as the forgotten names
of his victims flicker on the screen. "Like you, seek fame.
Find me, instead," he grins, pointing at the hero,
his twin, whose eyes are holes, whose mouth's a zero.

Ubi Sunt?

How I miss the senile widow
shouting "Who are you?" each spring
when I washed my storm windows,

and the deaf diva down the street,
who yelled into her phone in German
like Brunhilde in *Die Walküre*.

Renters live in her house now.
They've swept the carved cows from her mantle,
making room for their beer bottles.

Where's my neighbor's redbud tree
whose heart-shaped leaves once masked green siding
which now fills my study window?

Where's the maple which once screened
the intersection's four-way stop sign
until the city chopped it down,

but which also blocked my view
of the abandoned, paintless house
which stares at me when I look up?

Where's the mortgage, now paid off,
that once drove me to take bad jobs
in distant cities to make money

instead of watch decay at home
and groan for everything that's gone
like some bourgeois François Villon?

But whining over lost good neighbors,
blighted houses, cut-down trees,
distracts my thoughts from the decline

that stares me in the face each time
I step out of my steaming shower
and wipe mist from my shaving mirror.

Who's that spectre slapping lather
on my cheeks with bony fingers?
He's the Ghost of Present Tense,

although he haunts the past and future.
When he brandishes his razor,
I grin and offer him my throat.

2

ARRIVALS

Arrivals

1. Domestic

Drop your bags, flick on the television,
bounce test the mattress, strip, pad to the bathroom,
twist the bathtub's knobs until you learn
the secret combination of hot water
(standardized in every other aspect,
each motel room's faucets are unique),
shower, wrap your head and waist in towels,
and stroll around your walls admiring prints
of Mexicans asleep beneath sombreros.
Lie down. Calculate the hundreds or thousands
of miles to where you come from or are going.
Open the Yellow Pages to "Restaurants."
Sneer at the words "authentic" and "cuisine,"
shudder at "Cookin'" and "Since 1956."
Isn't there a half uneaten sandwich
wedged in the bottom of your flip-top cooler,
or six months worth of frequent flyer nuts
squirelled in your trench coat's secret pocket?
Flip to channel 20, The Weather Station.
Watch the saw-toothed cold front from Alberta
rip through tomorrow's path. You could hole up
here one more day and let the storm pass over.
The thought turns your blood to ice. You scan the dial
until you find the all-night Creature Feature
and lull real fear to sleep with movie terror.

2. Foreign

Can any room this small cost 80 dollars?
Wallpaper flowers, lace curtains, absence of screens
in a continent swarming with flies and lightning trains
that cruise at a hundred and fifty miles per hour—
which century is this, the 18th or 22nd?

Those bloody spots on the ceiling are squashed mosquitoes;
tonight will be your turn to close the shutters,
stand on the rickety bed and swat them flat
with a rolled up *International Herald Tribune*.
But now, lie down, allow your head to spin
with the merry-go-round rotation of the earth.
Remember your night spent drifting through the clouds
with a pointless movie flickering on the bulkhead
of the tourist cabin like a shared bad dream.
When you close your eyes you can still make out
the noiseless car chase scenes and silent blasts
you watched long after you pulled your earphones out
of the multi-lingual console in your armrest.
In the few short intervals of dialogue,
where men spoke to before they shot each other,
you read their lips in English, tried to guess
just how "You're dead meat, sucka" sounds in French,
Italian, German, Dutch and Japanese—
and then the earth's horizon dipped below
the sun which mercifully blanked out the screen.

3. *Home*

Look! It's not a smoking ruin! The trees
have grown yards taller and the street has narrowed,
and a station wagon's stolen your parking space,
but otherwise the place appears unharmed.
The blinded windows stare their vacant stares
at you as if you were a Fuller brush man
clutching a load of samples in your suitcase.
The front door doesn't fling itself aside
as you stand before it fumbling pockets
for the key you haven't slipped into the lock
for so long that, when finally you find it,
you forget for a second which way to twist it.
Just a minute. Think before you slip it
in and send that nerve shock through your hand
that sparks your motor memory and destroys

the strangeness of this place, so long a habit,
but, through the magic of your absence, changed
into a stop on your itinerary.
The crockery, the mantle junk, the TV
crouch behind that door, waiting to spring
like a family of clutching children, screaming
YOU'RE HOME! That's not living—that's routine.
Oh how it drags your swinish body in.
But your pilgrim soul flies up the chimney
as you relight the hearth of this feeble shrine.

Pilgrimage to Haworth

Jostling for a space to read the sign
describing Emily's death on the divan
roped off out of reach of Brontë fans,
I wondered if the 40,000 corpses
in the churchyard framed by their playroom window
had poisoned the brilliant sisters' air and water
or if they'd died, like their quiet neighbors,
of damp and cold and lack of central heat.
Before their books put Haworth on the map
the Brontës' town was famous for its death rate—
the shortest life expectancy in England
according to the sign inside the church
where I'd begun my tour, in search of tombs
obliterated a century before.
Instead of "Here Lie Emily and Charlotte"
and deathless praise carved in their monument,
I'd found a plaque fixed to a side aisle column
whose footing pierced their vault and crushed their bones.
The parson who'd replaced the Brontës' father
had raised a new church on the old foundations.
Claiming that the dead had undermined
the antique floor, he sealed it with concrete,
but his hygienic layer proved too thin
to separate dead writers from live readers.
Many of them stood where I stood and groaned
at reasons offered why the little preacher
didn't simply leave the old church standing
and build a new one on the ample grounds:
to cut construction costs, and to preserve
links with the past he added his new nave
with unobstructed views of his new pulpit,
to the ancient steeple, which he saved.
That cross-tipped phallic needle pointed skyward
at cloudless blue as blank as Arizona's
when I stepped out again, after shuffling
past every relic in the Parsonage—

Emily's tippet, Charlotte's doll-sized gown.
The lung-destroying damp and gloom I'd sought
had eluded me like early death,
and the only proper-looking ancient tombstones
I'd come across were Catherine's and Heathcliff's
plaster movie props from *Wuthering Heights*.
Clutching my 10 cent trail guide, I set out
across the dusty moor toward "Heathcliff's house,"
which turned out to be an abandoned farm
surrounded by a flock of sheep. Like them
I sought shade from the fierce sun and found some
in the shadow of a broken wall.
When I tore open a bag of salted peanuts,
they nudged me, baa-ing, till I threw them some.
Sharing lunch with these un-sheepish sheep,
I sat there listening for the "wuthering" wind
but heard only the crunching of our jaws.
"Are peanuts good for sheep?" I asked. "Beats grass,"
they answered, nudging me for more. Regret
that I'd been robbed first of the Brontës' tombs,
then of the windy rain that killed them young
struggled with content in my sheep's heart
as I munched with my comrades in the sun.

Angel Sighted from Airliner!

Flying over archipelagos
of icebergs curved in hundred-mile-long commas
radiating south from glacial cliffs,
I remember reading in *World Geography*
that Greenland's smaller than it looks on maps.

The winter sun streamed through eastern windows
of the overheated classroom, stirring flies
and falling in a trapezoid of glare
across the page that showed Adelie Penguins
diving off a floe into ice water.

Their white-rimmed, manic eyes dared me to flop
naked with them into the pale blue sea
shadowed by clouds and passing airplane wings.
The radiator hissed; the hatched flies droned;
dust motes chased each other in the sunbeam.

I slipped my school tie off, untucked my shirt,
stepped out of saddle shoes and blue serge pants,
and stood among the penguins, just their height,
pudgy, awkward, in cotton socks and briefs.
But at the lip of the floe a thunderclap—

a ruler cracked against my oak-topped desk—
retrieved me from the brink. My penguin friends
cackled as I woke and took five licks
across my palm that taught the difference
between the real world and my land of dreams,

which lies below these silver airfoils, now,
blue and white, horizon to horizon.
"Greenland looks ten times its actual size
because of its far northerly position.
Its name's deceptive too: It's white, not green!"

I wrote those sentences one hundred times
between thick lines of my marbled notebook
while my freed brain wandered to the ceiling
to peer down on my second grade companions
reciting Capitals and Industries:

"New Jersey, Trenton, oil refineries";
"Oregon, Salem, lumber and paper mills";
"Maryland, Annapolis, fisheries and steel";
they droned, the boys' hair stiffened with Vitalis,
the girls' hair tied in pony tails or braids.

I buzzed along the ceiling with the flies
looking for the exit through the neon.
Below my throbbing wings my classmates ranged
in rows and columns like squares of wheat and corn,
and I was one of them, hunched at my task:

To write the truth about deceptive Greenland
over and over and over and over and over
until I found the pinhole and crawled through
the school roof to the other side of life.
Like a cicada, my husk stuck to the seat

behind John Barker, in front of Bob Travere,
who've risen from their places too, by now—
filed forever out the double doors
splintered years ago by a wrecking ball.
Our teacher died; her soul, freed of us, soared

way north of boring latitudes of fact.
She's cloudy white, floating above ice islands,
unmarked on the Titanic's chart, which don't
exist until they rip truth's bottom out
and drown us. She flies with me in Greenland now.

Room with View/Radio

Twisting plastic knobs, I search
up and down the dial for music
but tune in only news in German,
incomprehensible to me
except for names of politicians
in Geneva talking peace
while their armies shell civilians.

Far from *Frommer Guide Book* cities,
I've learned to translate gibberish
in railway cars and can predict
just when a whining Spanish child
will drive its mother to lash out,
and which Czech couples will divorce
by the contempt that dulls their voices.

Last night, I "talked" for fifteen minutes
to my monolingual landlady
by saying "ja" each time she paused.
"You Americans are dopes!" "Ja, ja,"
might have been our dialogue,
but she charged so little for this low room
with its grand view of Alps, I think

she said, "When you wake to all this beauty,
look *up* before you jump from bed."
But even if she'd spoken English
I'd still have nearly knocked my brains out
against the ceiling beam, just now,
as I kicked off the quilt and stood
to get a better look at icecaps.

They swam like clouds until I blinked
to focus them in my pain-blurred vision.
They're solid barriers of ice
which block the sunrise from the valley

and which reflect all FM beams
back into outer space except
this local one that echoes off them.

This signal's trapped within these mountains,
so every quarter turn, I tune
the same announcer's toneless voice
re-reflected through the spectrum,
not the symphony by Mozart,
Beethoven, Bach, or Brahms I search for
to underscore this painful grandeur.

Feeling for the power switch
to shut the flow of chatter off,
I accidentally up the volume
so that the speaker shouts in German
about partition of a country
on border lines first sketched by tanks,
then inked in later on a treaty.

This news seems, strangely, to make sense.
Though I recognize just names of towns
made famous by their recent pillage,
and surnames of the politicians,
though not what faction's led by which,
I take in treachery and lies
as if I'd spent years at Berlitz.

Twisting dials, I manage to tune
faint violins through an Alpine gap.
Tschaikovsky? Maybe. All that comes through
crackle and hiss is the composer's sadness
before the weak signal's pushed out, again,
by news of genocidal war
in language more universal than music.

Caliban and Ariel

Parachutists circled down
toward pastures thick with grazing cows
inhaling grass with sucking sounds
that I could hear from yards away,
hiking a path that crossed the valley.

I picked out an aqua chute
from dozens of yellow ones and tracked it
the way, as a child, when I blew a stream
of bubbles from a bubble wand,
I'd follow one until it popped.

But looking up at the falling chute
instead of down at the rising path,
I stepped in a slippery cow pie,
turned my ankle, lost my balance,
and landed hard in soft, wet grass.

The nearby cows gave me the eye
but didn't stop chewing as I got up,
soaked, stinking, with a throbbing foot,
and muttered at their careless habit
of flopping anywhere they felt like.

Then I remembered the aqua chute,
looked up and scanned the empty sky—
nothing wafting on the wind but clouds—
then spotted it far down the mountain,
pale blue drifting past the green of pines.

I saw the shrouds that tied the harness
to the arching canopy of silk,
which, tugged this way and that, controlled
its speed and angle of descent,
though no maneuver could make it rise.

"That's the trouble with this sport,"
I muttered as I watched her drop—
I guessed it was *her* by the yellow braids
that sailed straight out from her crash helmet—
down towards steadily munching cows.

Unconcerned by the human rain,
they lolled their heads while I stood, tense,
worried they'd get the milk scared from them
if that parachutist landed wrong
and gored herself on innocent horns.

But seconds before her boots touched down
on Bossy or Flossy's bended neck,
she tugged the cords and sheared off
into a patch of cow parsnips,
landing soft as a meadow lark.

I heard her whoop with joy and triumph,
and I whooped too, from sweet relief,
but the cows ignored the miracle
my eyes were glued to as I limped on
through shit-strewn pasture ducking angels.

Kearney, Nebraska

An eighth of a mile from the Interstate that links
New York with San Francisco there's a choice
of rooms with King-sized beds or Double Queens.
The Budget Inn costs more than The Luxury,
but both take pets, like all motels in town,
so after dinner at a AAA approved
restaurant featuring American cuisine,
guests can lie down with animal companions
and listen to trucks shift gears and barks and yips
of fellow travellers' dogs through wallboard walls
until their air conditioning fan kicks on
with a steady rumble swallowing all sounds
like the *ooom* of meditation in Tibet.
Midway between Grand Island and North Platte,
between the prairie and the Rocky Mountains,
between the Lincoln Tunnel and the Golden Gate,
the town's innkeepers and restaurateurs expect
their patrons to eat and sleep and drive away
next morning, so the menus never change,
since no one ever dines out more than once,
but every bed gets fresh sheets every day
to make sure pets don't pass along their fleas.
When, now and then, someone does not check out
after complimentary donuts at the office,
the clerk at the reservations desk gets nervous—
did a Senior die of a coronary?
or a discouraged salesman cut his throat?—
not guessing that a transient might stop
halfway between departure and arrival,
with hundreds or thousands of miles to go, for pleasure.
But weary check-ins from the East must lose
momentum when their knots of fear untie
as killer cities shrink in rearview mirrors
and their windshields fill with fields of wheat.
And every Westerner must feel the urge
to stop here where the big blue bowl of sky

isn't chipped by mountains around its rim
and where the smog-free air is so transparent
the only way to know that it exists
is to steer through it when it's blowing crossways
from pole to pole, filled with cranes in flight
from Canada to Mexico in fall
and Mexico to Canada in spring,
who stay six weeks, fattening on grain
before they take off into the wind again,
waving their enormous wings good-bye.

Space Walk

This morning, when I gave up trying to sleep
and snatched my Rand McNally book of road maps
out from underneath my curled-up cat
to take a mental trip somewhere not gray
as the dawn clouds and her thick winter fur,
I found the Eastern U.S. clawed to bits.
That left me just the desert west of Kansas
to trace my way to with my index finger
while my brain remembered or created
blue sky and a landscape flared with sun.
But imaginary driving's complicated
because I can't start out from where I live
five inches right of center, now in tatters.
I'll have to leave from someplace like Topeka,
just left of the staple in the map,
and add a day's drive over shredded roads.
But freezing drizzle's just begun to fall,
so I'll have to crawl behind a plough
that kicks road salt into my iced-up windshield.
The extra hours I'll drive after dark,
my fingers welded to the steering wheel,
will cure my usual insomnia.
The complimentary donuts will be gone
by the time I check out of the Topeka Inn,
and I'll get snarled on Amarillo's bypass
around sunset tomorrow. On the third day,
just a thousand miles from where I started,
I'll wake at four A.M., jump out of bed,
and race to beat commuters to the beltway.
Then I'll aim my headlights at the moon
hung like a neon Exxon sign above
the empty Interstate. *Where to, traveller?*
El Paso? Albuquerque? Santa Fe?
They're too crowded, not far enough away.
I'll pull my wheel hard back and floor my pedal
until my car's nose lifts above the highway

and arches upwards towards that brilliant moon
high above the filthy atmosphere.
When I set down, I'll step out gingerly
in a silver-colored suit with silver boots
that leave the only footprints in the dust
as I explore those shadowy continents
and bright lagoons that I stare at on walks
on clear, cold winter nights in the empty park
a few blocks from my house—the one I left
at dawn in freezing rain, which turned to snow
that dusted frozen mud all silver-white.
Staring from the Moon towards the full Earth,
I'll yearn for my white speck, wiped out by clouds
swirling over Eastern North America
like Oleander's angry, twitching tail.
But once you leave the earth there are no maps
to show the way, or curl up on and snooze.
So calm down, kitty—here's the West to chew.
I'm stepping out to lay this world's first tracks.

Jetlag Aubade

When Alpine chapel bells rang out at dawn
the morning after I'd crossed the Atlantic,
I burrowed under pillows to shut out
my chalet window's view, although I'd squandered
two months pay to wake to mountain sunrise,
tinkling cow bells, and moos instead of smog-
hazed neighbor's houses and traffic noise.
Underneath two thicknesses of feathers
I tried to tunnel back into my dream
before my conscious mind switched on the lights
and all the guests at my fifth birthday party
evaporated in the brightening glare.

But memory's the cat part of my brain.
It hides in secret places when I seek it,
but whenever I lie down and close my eyes
it climbs in bed beside me, noses me,
then lays its needly paws on my shut eyelids
to make sure that I'm only playing dead.
So, instead of blowing out five dreamy candles
before they dripped wax on my chocolate cake,
then cutting a huge slice to give my girlfriend,
who clutched a pink-wrapped present whose pink ribbon
matched the ribbons in her yellow braids,
I lay in bed remembering all I'd lost:

my see-through plastic ruler/pencil sharpener,
my woodchip-studded first grade copy book,
my metal roller skates, my red tricycle,
my 48-piece U.S. Puzzle Map,
my Lincoln Logs, deluxe Erector set,
Tinker Toys, Monopoly, ball and jacks,
dump truck, jeep, plastic army men,
Cheerios Frontier Fort and Big Top Circus,
Lone Ranger silver gun and holster,
Howdy Doody mug for Ovaltine,

Captain Video code ring, cocker spaniel,
all my friends, my stepfather, and my mother.

I lay there stunned, as if I'd just clicked on
the bedside short wave, and BBC World Service
announced an earthquake centered on my house.
A minute before, feted by parents and playmates,
now orphaned, friendless. I stared up through the skylight
at fleecy clouds fringed by an unreal blue
as in a drawing of heaven by a child.
Then very, very gingerly I reached
beneath the goose-down quilt until I touched
something smooth and warm and soft beside me—
my lover's shoulder! I shut my eyes and tried
to keep on dreaming the dream that she was in.

Life Is like a Mountain Railway

Heaving backpacks on the luggage rack,
I plopped into the empty seat behind
the gurgling baby, whose coos would change to screams
when the locomotive revved its electric motor
and lurched our railway carriage up the Alp.
But, half dead from ten miles of mountain hiking,
and headachy from trying to translate foreign headlines,
waving from the hands of French and Germans,
announcing the Russian coup and death of hope
for liberal reform in Eastern Europe,
I'd hear just the whining dynamo
until the rumbling wheels rocked me unconscious
and I dreamed again of the flat Midwestern home
I'd flown across the Atlantic to escape,
which haunted my sleep like a persistent ghost.
The same delay between my mind and body,
months after I got discharged from the army,
made me return to barracks in my dreams,
where I was issued orders to Vietnam.
I pulled guard duty every night and woke
in a sweating panic with my fingers cramped
around the butt of the M-16 I'd cradled
against my aching shoulder in the dark,
until I took to staying up chain-smoking
with all night talk-show radio till dawn.

Now, I propped my head against the window
and dropped my eyes from Mont Blanc's glaciered peak.
The conductor signaled as a couple dashed
across the platform and hopped the moving steps.
Brushing past my knee out in the aisle,
they fell into the backwards-facing seat
behind me for privacy, I guessed—to make out,
as honeymooning Europeans do,
between unsatiating feasts of sex.
But, as I closed my eyes, instead of murmurs,

hard-edged phrases issued from their lips.
She asked for money. He claimed she'd spent too much.
She suggested they split up. He hissed
something lost inside the whistle's screech
as we plunged into a tunnel. Not sleepy now,
I pricked my ears like a soldier on night watch,
straining to filter out Italian babble
and baby howls from deadly hushed exchanges:
"I'll need at least five hundred pounds next week."
"I can't spare that much." Half overhearing,
half creating their whispered conversation,
I eavesdropped on their dialogue until
the train lurched to a stop and they got off.
I twisted my neck to take in her smooth beauty,
his middle-aged lined face so like my own
that when he whispered something that made her grin
and take his arm and kiss him lightly on the cheek
as they mounted the village street, I knew how much
he'd offered to keep her for another week.
And then some noisy Americans got on,
with COUP DEFEATED waving from their *Tribunes*,
and we resumed our progress up the mountain
with lovers reconciled and the world safe
enough for me to doze off to my nightmares.

3

SLOW

POISON

The Little Prince

Thanksgiving mornings, I envied orphans
who lived behind the chain link fence
in a mansion surrounded by an acre of woods
beyond the alley behind my row house,

whose tiny dining room filled up
with relatives bulging in ties and tight dresses
slapping cousins until they screamed
for spilling gravy on itchy new suits.

On television, Detroit Lions
would fight Chicago Bears for nothing
that mattered to anyone crammed at our table
eight hundred miles from both cities.

But all the men pretended to watch
during dinner to avoid talk.
Wanting to be a man, too,
I twisted my neck until it ached

to catch a glimpse of beefy linemen
tearing the heads off quarterbacks.
"Root for them to kill each other
so the Colts can beat them," said my brother.

What, in my head, I rooted for
was to discover my adoption papers
hidden in a drawer or closet upstairs
with a newspaper clipping attached:

"Carson Windsor and his lovely wife
tragically lost on the Matterhorn,"
or, even better, "missing servants
suspected of kidnapping infant Count."

But the last Thanksgiving I searched upstairs
for a hidden panel in my mother's dresser
while the family hooted and squealed downstairs,
I happened to glance at my chubby face

in her mirror and flinched. I thought it was hers—
that she'd caught me pawing through her things.
The lines of her cheeks and jaw imposed
themselves on my ten-year-old face like a mask.

Sadly, I closed the drawers and walked
to the window to stare through bare branches
of the oaks at the Tudor mansion they surrounded.
I pressed my face to the chilly glass

and peered towards its oriel windows.
In every bay, through leaded panes,
I imagined a child my age sneered back
at my row of squat, square, terraced houses

filled with children like myself,
scions of a mean inheritance,
while they, abandoned in baskets on doorsteps,
were free to invent their histories.

An hour before, on arrival,
my fattest cousin had charged out back
to hang from the chain links, yelling "Bastards!"
at shadowy figures threading the woods.

But, flattening my pudgy cheeks to the window,
I cried for envy of their bastard blood,
the aristocratic thinness of their hungry faces.
Then someone downstairs yelled, "Richard! Dinner!"

My juices churned, but I didn't go down.
The sound of my name revived my ambition
to become as royal as the orphans:
I'd *starve* myself into a king.

How Fiction Ruined My Life

Green-haired, inhumanly lovely, but
otherwise anatomically normal,
the extraterrestrial woman commander
of an intergalactic cruiser rescued
the hero of my favorite novel
from post nuclear war torn earth.
On the last page, as sunset flared
through twisted spires of Metroville,
she took his hand and ordered him
to climb the gangway of her space ship:
"Come vith us. Come vith *me*."

Her rich, contralto, alien voice
pronounced *w*s like *v*s
but showed no other trace of accent,
unlike the tall, strong girls at school,
who broadened their *a*s and *o*s, as I did.
All spoke our city's dialect
passed on by parents like a curse
except for the unearthly blonde
whose perfume dizzied me in class.
In a strapless green chiffon sheath dress
no other twelve-year-old on earth
could wear without a wired bra,
she didn't slur a syllable
when she asked me to do the *cha cha*
at our eighth grade Sadie Hawkins dance.
My life up to her invitation
flashed through my mind as if death's claw
had hooked my wrist, not her slim hand,
and led me out onto the floor.
I ransacked memory for the reason
she'd picked me but could think of none:
tall for my age, but overweight,
I wasn't strong or swift or tough,
but also wasn't scarred or hunchbacked

so as to give her choice the merit
of Beauty's kindness to the Beast.
Stiffly prancing back and forth—
one two three one two three cha cha cha—
I managed not to tread her toenails,
painted red in red high heels,
and when the music stopped I thanked her
and staggered back to a knot of pals.
They grinned and poked my sides with elbows
as I would have if they'd been picked.
But their guffaws embarrassed me.
Now that I'd been raised off earth
and spun in orbit for three minutes,
I couldn't bring myself to laugh
at dirty jokes as we walked home.
Like Bernadette stunned by her vision
of Virgin Mary in the movie
shown in the gym the week before
with Mary played by Linda Darnell,
"Hollywood's most flawless beauty,"
I stumbled home through grimy streets
flanked by my companions, wondering
why she had picked unworthy me
to change into an alien
whose mission was to spread the worship
of Beauty in this ugly world.

"Her slender hand imprisoned his.
She led him up the laser ramp
into the belly of her craft,
whose ion thrusters hummed and throbbed.
'Any regrets?' she asked as he
looked away from his blasted planet,
receding in the viewing screen,
into her shimmering, orange eyes.
'None,' he mouthed. The roar of thrusters
drowned his reply, but she understood
and covered his trembling lips with her own."

Why I Have No Children

When I turned twelve and feared I'd go to hell,
I used to write lists of my mortal sins
on paper scraps I tucked into my wallet.
Each time I broke one of the big commandments—
not little ones, such as to honor parents
which even Jesus, like me the son of peasants,
had never really managed to obey—
I'd score a mark next to the sin's code name.
ITA meant Impure Thoughts and Actions,
which, I was told, were what was forbidden
by Thou Shalt Not Commit Adultery
and Thou Shalt Not Covet Thy Neighbor's Wife.
ITA got almost all my slash marks,
like the front runner in a landslide election.
Although I treaded ants and swatted flies
I never checked the K for Shalt Not Kill.
And though I coveted my neighbors' goods,
such as the boy next door's Deluxe Parcheesi,
I never stole, but only begged and whined
until I got the stuff I really wanted—
everything except the model airplane,
marked "$10" in the dime store window,
which really flew, and burned real gasoline.
All year I hoarded lunch and candy money,
then, on my birthday, my rich uncle Tony
doubled my life savings with a five.
Abe Lincoln's kindly portrait seemed to say:
"You're free, boy. What you want is yours."
I waved the bill and danced a jig of joy.
And then, out of the blue, my mother said,
"That plane's dangerous. I won't let you buy it."
"Godamn you to Hell I hate you!" I spat out
and ran up to my room and slammed my door
and barricaded it with a chest of drawers.
Even now, as I write down my curse,
I shake with rage. What I remember best

of eighteen years of living with my mother
is the one thing she wouldn't let me buy,
not even with my own hoarded money.
I dreamed, again, last night of that plane.
I laid my crisp new five and wrinkled ones
and quarters, nickels, pennies and a dime
on McCrory's shiny counter, and the clerk
with hooks instead of hands clawed up my cash
and punched ten dollars in the register,
and everything I'd been denied was mine,
until I woke and remembered my dead mother.
This is my confession of the sin
I never marked down on my childish list.
I doubt that it will ever be forgiven.

Front Porch Visiting

On the nursing home's front porch
swathed not in wool, but air
smudged by global warming
to an even, tepid gray,
I'll think of cold blue days
like this one with nostalgia.
Wheeled out of my room
for "sensory stimulation,"
and issued a docile cat
to cradle in my arms,
I'll look straight at the sun
through gasoline haze and remember
today's wintry glare
falling on this page
so brightly I have to shade it
with my left hand as I write.
And I'll remember the feisty cat
rolling on my lap,
her licorice-colored fur
turned chestnut by warming light
which drugs her defenses so that
I can stroke her unguarded white belly.

Ranged on that porch beside me,
strapped into their wheelchairs,
my tranquilized companions
will stare, like me, at the sun
while chatting with dead husbands
and wives about dead friends.
I'll overhear their halves
of intimate conversations
as I have at public phones—
pleading or angry voices
transmitted over black wires
to invisible listeners
whose inaudible replies

stir terrible emotions sometimes.
Waiting to call a tow truck,
I've eavesdropped on jilted lovers
sobbing into receivers
and viciously low-pitched voices
threatening hearers with death
while I shifted from foot to foot,
and the dimes in my palm grew hot.

But calls from that future porch
placed very, very long distance,
will require my companions to speak up
to be heard on the other end.
Even with my deafness,
I'll intercept their messages
to the dead as I did in childhood,
sprawled on my front porch,
when the widower next door sat
at his table with two glasses of beer
and muttered to his dead wife.
His voice rose in argument
while I bounced my ball and swept jacks—
onesies, twosies, threesies—
and listened for her replies.
I couldn't hear her talk,
but when he went in I peeked
over the ledge that divided
our connected row house steps
and saw that her glass was drained.
So I knew she'd returned from the dead
to silence his complaints.

They quarreled on their porch all summer
as they had the summer before
her heart attack and funeral.
And then, that fall, their daughter
took him to a "home."
My mother said he was crazy
talking to himself like that,

but I knew he wasn't. I learned
to hear her side of their talks
as I lay flat on the concrete
behind the ledge and listened
to her indignant denials
that she wasted money on doctors
and kept a filthy house.
"I'm too sick to scrub floors,"
she said, as she had in life,
and he grumbled, "no, you're not,"
as if she hadn't died to prove it.

Between that haunted porch
and the haunted one in my future
everything I love
will have turned into a ghost,
even this winter sun,
which has put the cat to sleep.
The shadow she casts on this page
prefigures the gray afternoons
I'll sit with dying strangers
mumbling to our dead lovers.
But they won't come to us
as Lilly did to Chuck
next door, when I was six.
They'll cling to their clear black vacuum
sucking us toward them
on the other side of the veil
of smoke shrouding our planet.

Adult Education

Slumped in their desks like hostages
to Arts and Science Core requirements,
when asked "do you like French?" in French
my classmates spit out, "*Je déteste.*"

I see our teacher's bland young face
absorb their gleeful ignorance
while I prepare to cheer her up
by mumbling *J'aime parler français.*

But lazy lips give me the accent
of a Saturday Matinee movie cowboy
parlaying Frenchy with Belle and Mimi
as he sips whiskey in the Long Branch.

Those Westerns taught me Spanish, too—
as spoken by grinning banditos to gringos
who mangled it to "Vamoos, amigos,"
and "Hasta la veesta, seenorita,"

waving good-bye to Yvonne DeCarlo,
who wept as they remounted stallions
and galloped north to the Rio Grande.
God I envied their sophistication.

One Monday recess, caught trying to *hablo
español* with Juanita Daide
instead of shooting basketballs,
I was severely warned by a nun:

"that Hollywood junk will rot your brain."
But in what tongue was she fluent?
Her Latin might help me cross the border
into the distant country of death.

But, once my corpse had been anointed,
I'd never get a chance to speak it,
because, in hell, I'd only scream
or else, in heaven, so many'd sing

that I could fake Gregorian chants
by lip-synching the *Glorias*
just as I mouthed hymns silently
to not mess up the girls' choir voices

drifting down from the hidden loft
which, my first time in church, I thought
were angels singing angel language—
all high-pitched, universal praise,

no guttural mutters to pass the food
such as filled the vocabulary
I learned and spoke at family meals
I bolted at the kitchen table.

Later, my range of English expanded
with mispronounced words I learned from books,
but my Spanish speaking skills dried up
when the Rex Theater became a porn-house.

And years of high school French destroyed
all desire to speak it forever,
I thought, until, one day last month,
staring at my souvenir wall map of France,

then out my window at a porch-full of Hoosiers
in caps set sideways, sipping Bud,
I suddenly wanted not to live
here all my life in ignorance.

That's how I came to this front row seat
in the night section of F100,
required of my classmates—but I could be home
watching Cisco and Pancho on cable TV.

Mais je préfère mon cours de français
I stumble out to our teacher, who smiles
at my hopeless accent. "*Très bien,*" she lies,
and I tell myself I'll die in Paris.

The Thinkers

Hunched naked by the art museum,
the birdshit-spattered "Rodin's Thinker"
drew hoots from us high school commuters
each time we rode past on the bus

on our way to Baltimore Polytechnic.
In fall we'd thrust our heads out windows
and holler something witty, like
DON'T FORGET TO FLUSH THE TOILET!

When snow peaked on his head in winter
we said he wore his Thinking Cap,
and when spring melted it we laughed
at pigeons roosting in his hair.

But up the marble stairs he flanked,
the big bronze doors protected statues.
The Renaissance to Early Cubist
nudes were sheltered from guffaws

in guarded rooms I never entered,
not even on the Students Free Days,
though, once, I spent my month's allowance
and cut Math class to catch the striptease

matinee at the Gaiety.
The featured dancer, Gaye Purree,
made love to air on a velvet couch
while I watched, in reverent silence,

though I'd come to hoot with friends.
Up in the balcony, bums snored
while in the pit the yawning drummer
pounded elemental rhythm

she thrust her hips to—DUM da DUM.
Bathed in ruby, then blue light,
she glowed with artificial beauty
like a figure carved from lapis lazuli.

She writhed and wrapped her slender arms
around her phantom lover's back,
raking it with long, black nails
manicured to look like claws.

When she purred her trademark purr,
the boys I sat with poked my ribs
and whispered jokes about good pussy,
but I hissed, *shut up and watch*.

Afterwards, I rode the bus
in silence as my pals repeated
dirty lines the burlesque clowns
had shouted at the heckling house.

Wrapped in talk or thought, we passed
"The Thinker" without remark for once.
Ignored instead of scorned, he brooded
next to the art museum's steps,

mulling, in his metal brain,
how skin impresses more than bronze
as a representative of flesh.
The thought froze on his rigid lips;

he couldn't shout it at my bus,
which puffed a cloud of blue exhaust,
obliterating him in smoke.
But decades later, when I saw him

in Rodin's Paris garden, perched
above the Gates of Hell, I heard
him speak these words inside my head:
better here than Baltimore.

His feet were welded to this sign:
ABANDON HOPE ALL YE WHO ENTER,
and sculpted under him, the Damned
writhed in artful agonies.

Incident at Third and Woodlawn

The flaming trees, like girls on prom night dressed
in orange and gold they'll change to gray tomorrow,
distract me as I step into the street.
A horn, a brake, a turning driver's scream—
I dodge her bumper, hopping to the sidewalk,
luckier than that squirrel laid by the curb.
He's flattened, abstract, except for his glassy eye.

Meeting his stare reminds me I've been struck
down twice by cars. Once, looking neither right
nor left, I raced toward Carol Anne's yellow curls
bobbing on her neck across the street.
When I woke up, unhurt, one whole day off
from grade school with an x-ray of my skull
for a souvenir, I said I'd learned my lesson,

but twelve years later, many states away,
musing on the date I hustled toward,
I got knocked down again, by a swerving teen
on her first day of driving and my last
on earth, almost. Looking up I wondered
if stars I saw were real, or the kind you see
unconsciously in transit to your death.

They turned out real—the Big Dipper, Venus
glittering green beneath the crescent moon.
The stretcher crew so gently lifted me,
I sighed like a taken-care-of child.
Once more, x-rays showed no fractured bones,
and when I knocked, hours late, at my date's door,
my bruises turned her rage to sweet concern.

It's half a lifetime since her frown unwrinkled
in dim porch light to wide-eyed sympathy,
but I can see and feel that same change, now,
as sun breaks through a rift in mottled sky

and brushes my face like her unfisted hand.
The smiling sun and her gorgeous daughter-trees,
tossing down the favors of their leaves,

seem to love me as she seemed to, then,
loving, really, only my persistence
in trailing beauty like a bee in fall,
when threatening frost turns flowers into gems
and trees to flowers, and men in their forties
to squirrel brains. Oh Nature, take my hand
and help me safely cross to brown November.

Slow Poison

I dived into my house
just fogged with flea-killing bombs
to turn off a boiling pot
forgotten on the stove.
Holding my breath, I raced
across the living room carpet,
lunged into the kitchen,
extinguished the burner and ran
back out the way I came.
But my lungs, still brittle from smoking,
though I quit ten years ago,
burst in my chest as I clutched
my doorknob, and I gasped
before I could push outside.
Exhaling the stinging stuff,
I crouched on my doorstep coughing
and blinking my watery eyes
the way, years ago, I did
in the army gas chamber drill,
where I had to unmask and breathe
enough CS to wince
before they let me escape.
But, rooted deeper than pain,
a strangely pleasant feeling
stirred inside me. The bug spray
had kicked like nicotine
the first time I inhaled.
At five I'd begged my stepfather
to give me a puff of his Camel,
and when, for a joke, he did,
I'd sucked the smoke straight in
instead of mouthing it like him.
"Oh, Jesus," he said as I choked
and gasped, red-faced, for air.
But when I recovered my breath
and said, "gimme another puff,"

he laughed and shook his head.
"Cigarettes will kill you,"
he said as he lighted up
another and dragged deep,
"but a little whiskey's all right.
Don't tell your mother about this."
He handed me the dusty
half-pint of Four Roses he kept
in his toolbox for emergencies,
and I swigged the bitter stuff.
"Thanks," I said as I wiped
my mouth with the back of my sleeve
as he always did when he drank.
The burning spread inside me,
rising at last to my brain.
"I'm drunk," I said, and staggered
to bed for my afternoon nap
willingly for once.
And now, lying back
on my steps a lifetime later,
Stan's bones long in the ground,
I try to calculate
how much I've shortened my life
to save tonight's supper—beans
spiced with insecticide,
not good for you but delicious.
If Stan were here we'd eat them
with mustard and tabasco.
I make out his face in a cloud
drifting over the sun,
as I suck deep breaths of oxygen
to soothe my inward burning.

4

PICNIC

IN THE

BASEMENT

Picnic in the Basement

For the last time this year I clip
what's left of the stunted elm hedge—
brown gaps in it like rotten teeth.
Then I heave the picnic table
no one's eaten at all summer
onto my shoulders, like Atlas, and stagger
through the garage to the black basement,
stumbling over the broken trellis
that held the climbing rose that died
the month after I moved here.
I reach for the wall to steady myself
and grab a handful of plastic pickets
I bought to fence the vegetable garden
I sowed that first year with lettuce
whose leaves tasted bitter as weeds.
The table slips and luckily falls
away from the wall of flowerpots
filled with geranium skeletons
blighted by frost last September,
and lands in the center of the concrete floor
an inch from my foot. I set it upright,
slide one of its splintery redwood benches
to elbow-resting distance from it,
and, panting, take a seat. I'm finished
with outdoor living for another year.
I've oiled my push mower with the price tag
still attached from ten years ago
when I bought it downtown at the hardware store
converted to a savings bank
when the courthouse turned into a mall.
I've taped the orange power cord
slashed in six or seven places
where the suicidal trimmer trimmed it
almost in half but not quite.
I shudder whenever I touch its coils,
remembering the first time I plugged it in

to a living room socket and dragged it outside.
While I hacked the weedy hedge,
my cats nosed past the screen door
and wandered into the strange yard,
bordering a street of speeding cars,
hundreds of miles from where they were born.
When, finished, I wiped sweat from my eyes,
looked up, and saw the door ajar,
I rushed inside and ransacked rooms,
reached deep into closets and hidey-holes.
Finally, desperate, I ran out again.
Crying their names, I crawled the yard
at cats' eye level until—what joy!
I found them cowering under this table—
new then, half rotten now,
with its redwood paint bleached almost white.
That family picnic was our last.
Since then they've watched from kitchen windows
each spring when I haul the grill outside,
each fall when I haul it in again,
though I haven't cooked meat on it for years.
Now they're waiting for me upstairs.
I hear their claws click overhead
as they pace the kitchen, hungry, impatient.
Why not invite them to scamper down
the cellar stairs and join me here,
each with her plastic dish of Friskies
while I gnaw my bone of nostalgia?
I feel my way upstairs and fling
the cellar door open. Suspiciously,
they sniff their way down every stair,
while I slide the other bench
up to paw-resting distance
and set the largest pot of geraniums
over the table's umbrella hole.
It's safe here, sweeties, out of the glare
of the murderous outside world that's dying
for the eleventh time in eleven years.
Nothing's scary here but corpses

dragged in from the lawn and garden—
steel cutting edges eaten by weeds,
charcoal long ago flamed to ash,
and our ghostly centerpiece—
branching in your eyes of phosphorous—
flowers of death that bloom in the dark.

Do It Yourself

Changing oil to save ten bucks,
I smudged a twenty dollar shirt
with grease and blood from pinched skin
trying to twist the filter frozen
to threads that didn't budge until
I drove out to the Mall and bought
a Flexi-handle wrench from Target.
Then I slid under the front end,
locked a vice grip on the oil plug
and forced it in the wrong direction
until I stripped its nut. I lay
panting up at shiny metal
that I'd exposed by torquing steel
with leverage and all my might.
Then I locked on again and jerked
the right way, but the jaws slipped
and I barked my knuckles on the oil pan.
A drop or two of my fresh blood
fell on the twigs and leaves I lay on.
I gripped the nut again and slipped
and gripped and slipped until my hand
looked like the winner's in a fist fight,
so I paused to think. Shadows
chilled my legs that, when I started,
had been warmed by autumn sun.
My neighbor's yard light flickered on,
which meant that soon I'd need a lantern
I didn't own. An empty feeling
which must also have been felt
by three who waited for me upstairs
told me it was supper time,
time for me to go inside,
wash my hands and cook spaghetti.
Once in the kitchen I could dig up
from the coupon jar an ad for Quick Lube,
and let them do in ten minutes

what I'd been working on since lunch.
But how could they extract the plug
now that I'd rounded off its edges?
Instead, I'd have to call the dealer
and make an eight o'clock appointment
to have a new drain hole drilled out
and the one I'd wrecked soldered shut.
"A hundred dollars labor plus
thirty for the oil and filter,"
I could hear the service manager
whisper in my mind's ear.
So I grabbed the vice with both hands
and squeezed till the veins in my wrists stood out.
The plug gave all at once and gushed
hot oil that washed my bloody fingers
black as it geysered into the catch pan.
My feet danced a little jig of triumph
which kicked over the fresh quarts
of oil I'd opened and casually set
in front of the bumper an hour before.
With a quick snatch from under the car
I wrenched my back but saved the quarts,
which, after I rescrewed the plug
and painfully stood up, I poured
into the engine, and I was finished
just five hours after I'd begun.
And then I limped inside to feed
my wife and cats and tell this story
of how, to be sure things got done right,
I did them myself and saved us money.

The Wedding of M & R (after Lucan)

> No witnesses except the gods attended
> their ceremony; no wreath hung from their lintel.
> —from "The Marriage of Marcia and Cato"
> in Lucan's *Civil War*

No witnesses except a courthouse clerk
on lunch break notarized their legal marriage.
No "best man" mutual friend, doomed to recede
decade by decade in their memory,
smirked as he fumbled for their wedding bands.
No bridesmaids dressed in organdy paraded
death march slow behind the flower girl
(bride's baby sister, soon to dwarf the bride)
who strewed no orange blossoms in the aisles
of a parish church demolished years ago.
An iron-rimmed glasses priest did not intone
love pledges like a Sunday litany,
nor did they drone back promises of faith.
Instead, a judge on recess from a trial
read cheerfully the ritual, less "obey,"
which they repeated loud and firm enough
for a clerk to swear in writing that they wed
on April 10, 1972.
Afterwards, they didn't kiss, duck rice,
drive to a hall where loud relations gathered
to tipple whiskey and dance to a polka band.
No bride's bouquet and garter, thrown and caught,
caused girls to blush and boys to snigger and snort.
She didn't wad a veil and gown in tissue
to bury in an heirloom cedar chest;
he returned no rented tux to Mister Penguin;
they didn't drive a tin-can dragging Chevy
to a Smoky Mountain Jacuzzi Sweetheart Cabin.
Instead, she caught a bus; he walked to work.
That night they drank champagne in a restaurant,
then, pie-eyed, staggered home and passed out.

Their unceremonious marriage, since that evening,
has proven fruitless in the legal sense;
no children and no custody disputes;
no property division, no divorce.
Nothing's come of their union but cats and books.
Justice, blind goddess, look elsewhere for your tribute,
for nothing will come of their dissolution
but one minus one, which makes your percentage zero.

My Muse

A rivulet of shower water rains
down on my face as I stare up at cracks
in the kitchen's ceiling beneath the bathtub's floor.
Through broken plaster I hear a mermaid sing
nostalgically about the salty spray that lashed
her body when she rode the wild waves free.
Combing her soap-drenched hair around her shoulders
must remind her of those centuries
she swam contentedly with fish and hummed
lyrics to herself which passing sailors
fatally mistook for cries of love.
I misinterpreted her song myself
that day I rowed by in my leaky boat,
but my keel was too shallow to scrape against
the underwater rocks that wrecked their ships.
I drifted close enough to hear her words,
not just the sweetness of her undertones,
so I was the first of her listeners
who didn't drown when I came to realize
that she was singing to herself, not me.
Somehow I seemed to know the words already,
and thoughtlessly began to echo them.
Years of singing above the moans of drowners
and castanet-like snapping of sharks' teeth
had deafened her to all tunes but her own,
but when she heard it bubbling from my throat
she dove from her sunny perch into cold waves
and swam out furiously towards its source,
straight and fast as a submarine's torpedo.
I huddled in the bow and tried to stop
singing but couldn't. My mouth and throat and lungs
compulsively repeated what I heard
not through my ears but from within my head,
while she homed on the sound, veering off
just inches from the planks I thought she'd ram.
She surfaced in a roiling pool of foam

and stared at me until my song began
describing her hypnotic eyes. She smiled,
shaping her thin lips into the V
that ancient island sculptors carved in faces
I thought they'd only dreamed. But no; they'd seen
hers—moonlit, marble white, grinning from the surf.
Like me they lacked a lying imagination
and only recreated what they saw,
which, luckily, was her. She smiled, I sang,
until a tidal wave caught up my boat
and beached us on this landlocked continent
a thousand miles from where our dirty river
flushes sludge into a filthy gulf.
I built this ark and waited for the flood.
But though the gray sky here has rained for decades,
year by year our overfreighted ship's
sunk deeper in the mud. She won't call it "home"—
she's an elemental goddess, not a goldfish—
but as I stand beneath the dripping ceiling,
it sounds like resignation's creeping into
her incessant weeping. She's singing, now,
that the shower's almost like wind-driven spray,
that the bathtub is a kind of minor ocean,
and, cheerfullest of all, that sure decay
seeping through my floor and roof and walls
means she'll only have to languish here a lifetime.

A Portrait of the Artist's Bedroom

Dirty glasses, coffee cups,
a VCR/TV remote,
and a shaky stack of books
crowd the night stand at arm's length
from the unmade, crumb-strewn mattress
set crookedly upon a box spring
whose claw-ripped undercloth sags down
from the weight of a sleeping cat—
safe, there, from the vacuum cleaner,
though it hasn't passed through lately
judging from the matted dust balls
clinging to discarded socks
wadded up like waste paper
tossed among haphazard shoes.
A trapezoid of winter sunlight
focused through frost-covered panes
illuminates a rumpled rug
off angle to the wooden floor's planks.
Dust, like snow, falls through the sunbeam,
slowly turning the black rug
and the pine-yellow floor light gray,
which is the color of the cat fur
scattered here and there in clumps,
some floating free, like tumbleweeds,
some clinging to the dresser's legs.
One of the dresser drawers, half open,
leaks white socks, jockey shorts,
and a slender, black tail—
don't close that drawer! Above the dresser
hangs a mirror framed in wood
with pictures wedged into each corner:
one of a black cat, one of a gray cat,
one of the two together and
a post card of Van Gogh's café.
The mirror mirrors two corner closets
across the room, their doors wedged open.

One's crammed with shirts and pants and sport coats,
one with dresses, skirts, and blouses,
half a dozen empty hangers,
and a tower of shoe boxes,
the three top ones turned on their sides,
open, stuffed with tissue paper
which shows the hollow where the shoes
nested till removed and packed
into the overnight bag which
isn't hanging from its nail.
Also in the mirror there's
the image of the sloppy bed
and night stand with details reversed,
and in the bed, in the real room
and in the mirrored one, there's me
with Nobody beside me, who
comforts us when she's away.

Some Terms in Real Estate Defined

"Gourmet kitchen" means two ovens
charred with cheese from frozen pizzas,
6 gas burners to boil water
for tea bags and instant coffee,
and a copper pot rack dangling
sauce pans stored with wedding presents,
unpacked and hung for the divorce
to jack this "custom" house's price.
"Custom" means not built of segments
hauled by semis labeled WIDE LOAD
to the building site and welded
side by side, then tied to stakes,
but, instead, framed up with presswood
sheathed in slabs of insulation
sided with strips of wood-grain vinyl,
shingled with squares of fiberglass
stapled to the "cathedral" roof.
"Cathedral" means a twenty foot drop
from the cork fake central beam
blackened to look like Tudor oak
to the "hardwood" "great room" floor.
"Hardwood" means eighth-inch parquet tiles
glued to concrete, and the "great room,"
built on the "open plan," combines
living/dining/family "areas."
"Open" means no walls or ceilings
with costly pipes and wires inside them;
"areas" substitute for all rooms
but the bedrooms and the bathrooms—
the "half," "three-quarters" and "full" baths.
"Half" bathrooms are sinks and toilets
crammed into remodeled closets;
"three-quarter" baths have moldy showers
poorly vented by loud fans;
"full" baths feature double sinks,
his and her gold plated faucets,

built in vanities, and mirrors
framed by Hollywood marquee lights.
Bedrooms which connect to bathrooms
are called "suites" or "master suites."
"Master" means a king-sized brass bed
faces a big screen TV
to watch instead of making love.
Downstairs in the "finished" basement
("finished" means floored with outdoor carpet
and walled with knotty pine veneer)
an imitation stolen beer sign
flashes "Bud" above the wet bar
no one's ever bellied up to—
no bottle ring stains mar its counter.
Nor has any body skied
the Nordic Track or trudged the treadmill
in the basement's "exercise room"
which leads to the three car garage
with room for only one car in it.
All the other space is taken
by the "workshop's" pegboard benches
piled with oily tools and scrap
making access slightly tricky
to the sliding door's UP button.
Stand tiptoe and press it twice.
Step outside to the "private" lot,
("private" means that 8′ fencing
walls the neighbors from a yard
that's "ideal for outdoor living"—
two decks and a new croquet set!)
Interested? Then make an offer
for this contempo mini-estate.
"Priced to sell" in the mid 250's
means it won't last long at that price;
only a quarter-million dollars,
and it might be gone tomorrow.

Decision at Silver Creek

Where asphalt stopped and dozer tracks began,
I parked beside the "Wooded Lots for Sale" sign.
I peered in the woods, searching for nuisance deer
who'd strayed from the state park, but found none.

Either the whining chain saws made them skittish,
or they remembered that their herd got "thinned"
this time the year before, when dry leaves fell
from branches they chewed, lacking other fodder.

Hundreds were shot to save them from starvation
and to protect their forest from destruction
Apparently it worked. No tooth marks scarred
the trees corralled by yellow construction tape

into pie slice lots around the cul-de-sac.
Although each lot sprouted a different sign,
I copied only the number on the one
that I could read while sitting in my car,

since all the lots were level quarter acres
equally covered with beeches, maples, oaks,
and several kinds of trees I couldn't name
because I've lived my whole life in the city

the way the deer have lived theirs in the forest.
They must know dozens of woody perennials
by their bark's scent, as I can name, blindfolded,
downtown's cafés by the smell of kitchen exhaust.

Sniffing my way to the Uptown, I'd smell Thai spice
at the Siam House, then Chez Nous' crème brûlée,
then follow the odor of Snow Lion's Tibetan tea
till I got hit by waves of Del Rio's salsa.

I knew, before "Closed for Vacation" got taped
to its menu board, that the Wok was killed
by competition from the new McDonald's
when I smelled the absence of soy sauce in the grease,

just as the deer can scent death in a tree
before its leaves curl up in early summer.
They're not shocked when it crawls with worms next spring.
If they could talk, they'd say something like,

"Old trees die to make room for new trees,"
as deer must die to make room for new deer,
and woods get cleared to make room for new houses
for people, like me, who're tired of city life.

Instead of looking out of grimy windows
at other windows, and hearing the roar of traffic,
I want to look at trees and hear bird calls,
and watch squirrels gather acorns. I'd be thrilled

if, now and then, a couple of browsing deer
strayed onto my lawn to nibble at my weeds,
provided they didn't carry Lyme disease,
and weren't so tame, or made so bold by hunger,

that they pressed their noses against my picture window
to look at me when I sat down to eat
in my dining room, which used to be their forest,
with a fire in my grate fed by their former trees.

Their hungry stares at my salad would spoil my dinner,
and they'd scar my eaves with antlers when they knocked
my bird feeder off its hook to spill its seeds.
They'd frighten my cats from their sills, and give them fleas.

"Something *must* be done to control those deer"
I read, with a shudder, in the *Herald Times* last year,
before I decided that I, too, wanted to live
in the woods where "their numbers are getting out of hand."

And something must be done again this year
to restore the balance of nature, which is terror
animals should feel at the scent of a man.
God knows I feel it. My instinct is to flee

to where no one is armed except deer hunters,
to replace the dark of the forest with my porch lights.
I only have to call this builder's number.
But I cross it out, and start my car, and *run*.

5

LIVING

IN

OBSCURITY

Living in Obscurity

Before I paused here on my way to Somewhere,
I'd lived by wave-torn cliffs and in the desert,
and in the South, where air's as thick as guilt,
and in the thin air of the vicious East.
Now, though the car I drove here's rusted out,
I still don't think of this place as home.
The locals glance at me and I at them
with the same quick, shy flicker of suspicion
today as on the day that I arrived—
not like the flare of hatred mixed with terror
that xenophobes exchange with immigrants
on city streets with no police in sight,
but like the flashing of strange lightning bugs
passing on their search for their own kind.
Yet, if not here, where *do* my kind belong?
I find them all the time in Roman histories—
the losing generals, exiled to islands,
raising sheep while editing their memoirs;
the villa-dwelling outcasts in retirement—
ex-contenders for the Consulship
Caligula conferred upon his horse.
Some of them, like Ovid, out of habit
kept begging for permission to come home,
but I think they were secretly delighted
to be kept from the mob that shredded Cinna,
mistaking him for one of Caesar's killers.
"I'm Cinna the poet, not Cinna the conspirator!"
he cried. "Then tear him for his bad verses!"
a jokester in the mob yelled, and they did.
Hours earlier that crowd had shouted,
"Down with tyrants!" and cheered Caesar's assassins,
whose houses it now sought to loot and burn,
but its dislike for poets has held steady
for several thousand years. No one would cry out,
"I'm a poet!" in a crowd today
except a mental patient labeled harmless

and cruelly booted from the state asylum
into the streets to save taxpayers' money.
Yet sometimes living here, so far from power,
I feel this strange urge to set up a booth
in College Mall out in the crowded aisle
between displays of Starcraft inboard boats,
huge as whales beached many leagues from water,
to sell remaindered copies of my books.
I see myself surrounded by tall stacks
of *Einstein's Brain* and *Alcatraz,* arranged
like B. Dalton's and WaldenBooks best sellers.
Now and then a passerby—a husband
bored with pricing riding mowers in Sears
while his wife picked shoes out for the kids,
a truant teen ducking school police—
would stop to poke around, lift up a book,
glance at my photo, put it down again,
while I leaned wearily against the counter,
checking my watch to see how many hours
I'd clocked at minimum wage, how many more
before I too was free to waste my time.
But if some loafer, looking at the cover,
noticed my resemblance to the Author,
I'd deny my own identity.
"I'm just paid to sell his books," I'd say.
"Would you be interested in one?" "No, thanks!"
my customer would say, and shuffle off
towards the big blue houseboat down the aisle,
leaving me anonymous, unread,
but safe, surrounded by a crowd that dreams
of sailing non-existent seas in Starcrafts
to ports unmarked on maps. Living here,
whenever one of us, lost in thought,
stops in a crowd, the rest part and regroup
silently, like ships around a rock—
no shoves, no horns, afraid we might wake up
and find ourselves in the Capital of Nowhere
exiled, forgotten, secretly satisfied.

Authors in Hell

It's hard to read dim pages lit by flames,
but movies, here, play at the porno house
which, since our bodies have been snatched from us,
taunts souls with big-screen sex. We do have brains—
or what, on earth, often pass for brains—
desire and memory. That's all we need
to make sense of the only books we read:
our own. Once able to endure the pains
tormenting us—the wheels and racks and chains
we hang from while God's vultures pick our livers—
we turn to literature. I float down rivers
of boiling blood, rereading *Einstein's Brain,*
my first and favorite book. I'd rather trace
its twisted lines in fire than live in grace.

Narcissus Experiences Technical Difficulties

"Please hold. Your call is important to us,"
says the computer, over and over.
From time to time the Voice suggests
that I press 1 and leave a message,
but since my VISA card's been charged
a thousand dollars for a sick computer,
I think I need to speak in person
to a person. While I'm holding,
says the Voice, I can press 2
to hear a Problem Solving menu
without relinquishing my place
in the line of people who need people
to tell their troubles to. I press 2.
The Voice instructs me to press *S*
for Software, *H* for Hardware, *U*
for Uncertain. I press *U*. She lists
common problems in a language
that sounds like Sanskrit, so I press
X to exit back to Hold.
"Please hold. Your call is important to us.
If you do not wish to wait
press 1 and leave a message.
If you'd like to hear some common problems
and their solutions without losing
your priority on hold, press 2."
I press the receiver to my sweating ear
as if to bring the Voice closer,
and whimper, "please" into the speaker
in case a person's listening in
on the computer's conversations.
Then a click and buzz and ring
like a one-armed-bandit's jackpot
tells me I've gotten through at last
to a human being who says, fast,
"Sales are final on that model.
You'll have to call the manufacturer

for the service center nearest you,"
and hangs up before I can say "but . . ."
So I call the manufacturer.
The Voice that answers says to press
L for laptop, *V* for video,
then estimates my wait will be
fifteen minutes for a person—
who turns out to be a non-native speaker.
But he talks slow, and I talk slow,
and soon we have arranged to fix,
no charge to me, at my house,
the broken screen of my bad computer.
"I switch you to dispatcher. Hold please."
I hold. The next voice that I hear
is Patsy Cline's ghost singing "Crazy,"
which sounds so good I'm almost sorry
when the dispatcher interrupts.
"Before we can repair your unit
we'll need a copy of your sales slip,
since our records show that model
is three years out of Warranty."
"But I just got it yesterday!"
"Do not worry, sir, we'll fix it
as soon as we receive your sales slip.
Just mail it in to this address . . ."
The line clicks, and I'm switched
to a Voice that spells a street in Texas
too fast for me to copy it
and hangs up. The line goes dead
as the dead screen of my computer,
which doesn't even reflect my face
now as I stare at its dull surface.
Mirror with a hole in it.
I meant to write thoughts it would flash back,
and read myself in its brilliance.
"Who do I call to make it do this?"
I moan into the dead receiver,
which echoes in my ringing ear,
"Who do I call, Who do I call . . ."

A Saint's Life

My mental pilgrimage to Santiago
keeps bogging down just past the Pyrenees,
where Spanish railway lines grow thin as threads
and strand me in a mill town *Michelin*
awards no stars to and *Real Guide* says to detour.
But when I reach for *Motoring in Spain,*
it warns that foreign cars involved in crashes
are impounded and their drivers jailed
until their case comes up in traffic court.
So I refold the road map and reach for
my *Thomas Cook's Timetable* once again,
searching for the railroad track that links
cathedral towns that El Cid liberated
while skirting 20th century industry
in grim Bilboa, Orense, and Gijon.
But the only way to do that is on foot
five hundred miles along the ancient path
whose barren swath's still visible through fields,
according to this article in *Travel*
which sent me to my guide books in the first place
looking for the easy way through Spain.
"Thousands walk the distance every year,
some for sport and some in search of faith,"
the caption says beneath a panorama
of pilgrims kicking dust up on the plain.
But judging from their grimly frowning faces,
I'd say they searched for what I'm searching for—
not God, or fun, which only kids believe in—
just variation from lead gray routine.
Boredom's held me hostage all my life,
and once I learned that alcohol costs more
in agony than it pays out in joy,
I started planning long, expensive trips,
then working overtime to finance them.
This cured my idleness for many years,
until I learned that every place is duller

than its blurb in *Frommer's* and *Let's Go.*
You might as well stay home, my heartbeat whispers,
as leukemia would whisper in my pulse,
you'll feel better, dead, than in such pain.
But when I listen, all I hear are trees
wildly howling in October wind
through all the windows of my narrow room.
Their red and golden leaves are taking off
in Spain's direction, though they're already dead
and therefore should be happy. Those restless leaves
show me the path I'll take to Santiago,
the air connections that my pilgrim soul
can only manage once it shucks my body,
martyred serving Differentness and Change,
and rises like burnt incense in Their worship
to cloud cathedrals built and wrecked in minutes.

Fiftieth Birthday

The towering forked maple down the street
screens nothing ugly out. I almost hear
the shacky house behind it cry for paint,
and through its wiry crown I see lead sky.
Each of its boughs and twigs runs crookedly
as an arthritic finger—useless lumber
if the coming spring wind blows it down,
or city tree men with a cherry picker
forestall its crash by chain-sawing it
to firewood logs from top to stump. No loss.

But when I squint, I make out fuzziness
that blurs the bony outlines of its branches—
buds! So it's not dead, just old and gnarled.
It's planning its next hundred thousand leaves
to paper over views of blight behind it
and to hide its twistedness beneath—
green lies, fluttering in June breeze;
stiff red and gold ornate ones in October.
Today, though, March 14, the naked tree's
forced to work with the truth. Against gray sky
its branches, slicked with drizzle, weave black lace
that decorates the gloom it can't conceal.

Portrait of the Artist as a Middle-Aged Man

for you know who

"The author now divides his time between
the American Midwest and southern France,"
it says below the fuzzy jacket photo
taken by his second or third wife.
But when I tilt the jacket toward the light,
this caption scrawled in secret ink appears:
"Divides" means teaching English on the Plains
ten months a year; two months of mangling French
in un-air-conditioned misery in Provence.
And when I trace the outlines of his face—
the out-of-focus wrinkles in his brow,
his dyed, receding hair and bridgework smile—
I measure both his true age and his urge
to shave a couple of decades off of it.
Before I open to the title page,
I know this new book won't be dedicated
to the same woman as his last one was,
and I can guess who'll get his "Special Thanks":
the editors and heads of grants committees
who've helped him get ahead most recently
or will, he hopes, assist him in the future.
"Acknowledgments" will list the magazines
he's cracked in the last six or seven years,
and finally will come his epigraphs—
a line of lyrics from a 50's hit,
followed by a few lines from Catullus.
Thin as it is, this little book feels heavy
as I turn the page to Section I,
"Childhood & Early Youth," and start to read
what crap he had to put up with in grade school.
I riffle through the pages reading titles
from "Salad Days" to "Sunset in *Camargue*"—
towards the end, there's lots of French italics—

and then I snap it shut. Before I toss it
on the months-thick stack of unread magazines,
I take another look at his masked face:
Mon ami! Mon frère! Moi in caricature.

Life at the Top

Since finding out that there's no heaven
in comparative religion class,
I've searched for earthly paradise
in tourist office info packs
like these, just sent from Colorado,
spread all over my knees and floor,
unfolded like maps of pirates' treasure.
I'm desperate to discover bliss
on earth before arthritis pain
or cancer make unconsciousness
the ecstasy I'm eager for
on my vacation in the tomb.
For, though I love a winter sleep,
it's knowing I'll rise at 4 A.M.
and walk the icy hall to the toilet
that makes me burrow under blankets
and hug my pillow like a lover.

Years ago, at a drunken party,
I fell in love with a woman who'd swallowed
a bottle of barbiturates
after tucking in her kids
one snowy night, the week before,
mistaking this urge to hibernate
as the urge to never wake up.
I asked how it felt as she drifted off
for what, she thought, was the last time.
"Wonderful," she said, breathily,
as if recalling romantic sex.
But later, counseling changed her mind.
She abandoned her children to her husband
and moved up to a mountain commune
where, she said, every day'd be great.
Or else she'd leap from a precipice.
Rolling down her VW's window
she kissed me good-bye the day she left.

Pursing her lips, she mimicked her shrink:
"I refuse to 'lower impossible goals
in order to get the most from life.'"

She never sent the promised post card,
so I don't know if she found joy
or leapt off a cliff, but others I cared for—
many then, nearly zero, now—
mailed me marriage invitations
then sad descriptions of divorces
for years before we lost touch.
None of them found the bliss they sought.
Or, if they found it, they picked it up,
held it to the light, tossed it away
like tenderfeet prospectors in the movies
stuffing their saddlebags with quartz
and tossing aside dull nuggets of gold.
Do they, like me, call toll free numbers
on February afternoons
on stolen breaks from tedious work,
requesting Chamber of Commerce packets?
Luxury Condos—Summer Rates . . .
Your Personal Rocky Mountain High . . .

Although I've wasted most of my life,
I might still rent an efficiency
or rustic cabin on Paradise Lake
and live for pleasure for two weeks,
or buy a vacation/investment dream home
with all I've saved by not living
like Beverly in her rattletrap Bug
who watched me dwindle in her mirror
until she reached the end of the street,
then downshifted and turned the corner,
leaving behind a faint blue cloud
of heady gasoline exhaust
I took a deep breath of, for remembrance.

Dressing for Work

Seven sport coats pressed together
elbow patch to elbow patch
make a dull rainbow in my closet,
seven shades of brown and gray.
I could sew labels on, like panties—
Monday, Tuesday, Wednesday, Thursday . . .
and wear a different one each day
if I were forced by staffing cuts
to work all seven days a week.
But chances are it's me they'll ax
the next time they slash the budget.
Then my jackets will hang useless,
since, when I'm not at the office,
I wear only jeans and sweatshirts
flung on the chair beside my bed.
Once I joined the unemployed
a thousand dollars worth of tweed
I couldn't pawn for more than ninety
would hang forlorn beside wool pants
and my collection of dress shirts
expanded every year at Christmas.
Then I could clothe a team of homeless
people as professionals,
but the fashion isn't warm
when cold wind blows through the lapels,
and in July the scratchy fabric
makes its wearer sweat and itch.
Costly, drab, uncomfortable,
my closet full of clothes for work
is only useful to disguise
the person in them as a drudge.
They camouflage, like the dull plumage
on small, defenseless birds who nest
on bare brown limbs backed by gray sky.
Their brown-gray feathers make them look
like twigs to hungry, circling hawks,

like clouds to little boys with sling shots,
like handsome fellows to each other,
sharing space at the branch office.
"Nice coat!" "Thanks." Says Tweety Sparrow
to Stanley Starling, who nods and blinks.
But Mr. Crow and Mr. Raven
in glossy all-black sharkskin suits
strut up and down, criticizing
all these little birds' mistakes.
The powerful are not "well dressed";
their huge, bare closets' hangers rattle
when they reach for cloaks and hoods.
No one ever praised the cut
of the Grand Inquisitor's black robe,
or said "nice wig" to a Lord Chief Justice
handing down a death sentence.
Only the weak dress up for work
in drab, expensive, useless coats
like these, so tightly squeezed in
I hardly can extract one
to wear with my new worsted pants
and buttoned-down, pinstriped, Oxford shirt.
I'm amazed how like a banker
I look in my bureau mirror,
but underneath, I'm naked skin,
and under that, a skeleton
which will be outlasted by
clothes too good to give the poor,
unlucky for the prosperous
to wear to their white collar jobs.
The coats will wind up in an attic
never wrinkled, never worn,
too dense for moths to get their teeth in.
This job of mine's depressing. Still,
it's nice to get survived by something.

The Education of a Professor

Desperate to escape the boredom
of Eighteenth Century Poetry
taught by a gray-haired World War II vet
who loved rhymed couplets, and wrote a few,
I quit grad school and joined the Peace Corps.
But, the instant I dropped out,
my draft board classed me 1-A.
I'd planned to teach in Liberia
while Lyndon Johnson bombed Hanoi,
and come back when the coast was clear,
but when Selective Service promised
I'd serve my two years in the army
now or after Africa,
I chose to fly home to the war.

But war, by luck, eluded me.
Safe in Georgia, I endured
boredom and humiliation
not much worse than in grad school—
which, after discharge, I went back to,
financed by the G.I. Bill.
Resolved to eat no shit, I dressed
in green fatigues among the tweeds,
and glared straight at the eyes of profs
in seminars when I remarked
that Pope and Dryden rhymed like Hallmark,
that Dickens pimped for the middle class.
My system worked. Professor X
scrawled "Forcefully Put, Mr. C,"
beneath his A on my indictment
of Virginia Woolf as an upper class twit,
and Doctor Y wrote "Funny, Original"
under my parody of *Paradise Lost*.
I picked my Ph.D. Committee,
breezed through writtens, breezed through orals,
applied for jobs in colleges,

and didn't get one. That was the year
Nixon pulled back from the war,
and all my hiding generation
came out from behind deferments
to compete with veterans for work.
But that same year, *Poetry*
published two of my bitter poems,
which fueled ambition and destroyed
my willingness to make a living
any other way but teaching
Remedial Writing and Composition
part-time in a junior college.
For ten years in three different states
I raised the level of competence
or lowered the level of incompetence
in Basic Skills for minimum wage
until, at last, I got a shot
at teaching a Lit course at Cal State.

But pupil's eyes glazed as I lectured
on "My Kinsman Major Molineux,"
until two sophomores wearing nose rings
came to my office to complain
that I rammed authors down their throats.
So I watered down the reading list,
eliminated James and Hawthorne,
and raised all of the Cs to Bs.
Meanwhile, inch by glacial inch,
my vita stretched with publications,
till, finally, I broke through
with a book of poems and a full-time job
as a one-year "Writer-in-Residence,"
where I tugged young poets up Parnassus,
though I'd barely dug a foothold, myself,
in its treacherously steep and slippery base.

Each year after that I scrambled
for Visiting Assistant Professorships—
the flinty patronage of states

replacing tenured retiring profs
with cheap one-year "renewables."
Learning to love the hunt for work,
for possibly better or fewer students,
I refused to be renewed.
I logged a hundred thousand miles
night driving rural Interstates,
tuning between the country stations
strongly beamed out of Missouri,
straining to hear, over engine noise,
the fading signal of Caruso
weeping while singing *I Pagliacci*
on PBS from Carbondale.
One dusk, in the delta of Arkansas,
a giant heron's silhouette
flapped across the sun setting
on a million acres of cotton fields.
"Jesus Christ! Wordsworth's right!"
I cried out, shaken by Nature's Beauty
as passionately as by Lust or Fear
for the first time in my life. I turned
to the seat beside me, where Wordsworth's ghost
adjusted his lap belt to fit over
his lumpy, outmoded frock coat.
He nodded gravely, pleased to admit
the last and least of the Nature Poets
to the dwindling circle of his admirers.
"Reread my *Prelude,* Friend," he said.

I did. And then I reread Shelley,
whose restless passion I'd mislabeled
"airy nonsense" in a paper praised
for "rough forthrightness" by Dr. Z.
Like Dante, in the middle of my life
I stumbled out of the Wood of Error
led by the shade of a great dead poet.
Traversing the *Norton Anthology*
page by page from Chaucer to Lowell,
I stumbled on buried masterpieces—

Dunbar's "Lament for the Makaris,"
Tichborne's "Elegy," Googe's "Of Money."
I laughed for the first time at Dryden's jokes,
and shivered at Wordsworth's "Ruined Cottage,"
as bleak and poignant as a Chekhov sketch.

Weeks after that heron crossed the sun,
I landed this job in the Big Ten,
teaching "Intro to Poetry"
to freshmen, freeing young professors
to teach Theory to Ph.D.'s.
While their seminars construct
approaches to works they don't read or like,
I dive and roll around in those works
like Disney's Scrooge in his vaults of gold
quacking, "mine! all mine!" One or two students
watch my antics with the intelligent eyes
of puzzled cats—they're my A+s.
On the rest I lavish As to teach them
not to hate what they don't understand—
the lesson this Bonehead English teacher
who wasted decades of education
learned in a flash and will teach forever.

Thanatopsis

after death there are two alternatives,
both heartless:
memory and forgetfulness.
    —Jon Anderson, "Creative Writing"

I glided sideways through my rib cage,
ducking and stepping high from habit
though I had no breakable skull or
stubbable toes to dash on bones.
Once outside, I spread my pinions
wide to hug the air kept from me
all my life by prisoning skin.
Doled out oxygen in breaths
taken by a swinish mouth
always swilling food and drink,
I had never felt real wind gusts
such as howled now through my fabric,
shredding me like a bubble blown up
inexpertly by a toddler.
My ideas attached to leaves
tumbling over sharp, dry grass blades;
my emotions, caught in updrafts,
quickly swept up to the clouds.
Only memory resisted
amalgamation with the elements,
clotting to a mercury droplet
while my rage changed into lightning
and my thoughts mixed with manure.
Mirrored outward from this droplet,
skeletons of trees danced wildly
underneath a blackening sky.
But inside its silvery surface
nothing flashed back but itself
in a billion glittering facets.
Spiraling dizzily I circled
galleries of portraits of me

fumbling footballs under street lights,
spilling beer in bowling alleys,
cheating on a high school French test,
slouching in limp green fatigues
while my sergeant ripped my stripe off
for reporting late to duty.
Hung inside the arching entrance
of the dome of friends and lovers,
my first date sneered from her frame,
while my grade school classmates grinned down
from the ceiling like crude putti
slapped up by apprentice painters.
Where's the room of Flemish masters?
I'd have asked if I'd had language,
not just images to think with.
Where's the charming wedding portrait
and the gems of genre painting
featuring cats on my blue plush sofa?
Staring down implacably,
teachers, bosses, rivals, critics
plunged their dagger stares through metal
atmosphere that held me like aspic.
Horrified, I tried to screen out
hostile images but had no
eyelids or fleshy hands to block them.
Lacking a mouth and tongue, I couldn't
cry out that my body's prison
was an airy nest compared
to the dungeon of my memory.
So I floated, dim and wordless,
past the hostile glares of children,
hurt looks of neglected parents,
teary eyes of those I'd slighted,
rising to a brightly curving
ceiling blank as untouched canvas.
"Let me out!" cried a lost hope,
yearning towards its friends in the clouds.
Then the roof became a skylight.
Through it, lightning lit the world

I could have if I would give up
all I'd been and known. I paused
long enough to feel regret
flash through me like burning niter
as I beat my wings and leapt
into the idiot serene.